DO THE WORK!
ZERO HUNGER

COMMITTING TO THE UN'S SUSTAINABLE DEVELOPMENT GOALS

JULIE KNUTSON

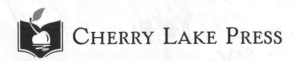
CHERRY LAKE PRESS

Published in the United States of America by Cherry Lake Publishing Group
Ann Arbor, Michigan
www.cherrylakepublishing.com

Reading Adviser: Beth Walker Gambro, MS, Ed., Reading Consultant, Yorkville, IL
Photo Credits: © addkm/Shutterstock.com, cover, 1; © panitanphoto/Shutterstock.com, 5; Infographic
From The Sustainable Development Goals Report 2020, by United Nations Department of Economic
and Social Affairs © 2020 United Nations. Reprinted with the permission of the United Nations, 7;
© addkm/Shutterstock.com, 8; © Sameoldsmith/Shutterstock.com, 9; © suheyptosun/Shutterstock.
com, 10; © Viktoriia Hnatiuk/Shutterstock.com, 13; © Pavlo Baliukh/Shutterstock.com, 14; © Digihelion/
Shutterstock.com, 16; © LightField Studios/Shutterstock.com, 19; © LADO/Shutterstock.com, 20;
© StunningArt/Shutterstock.com, 23; © Dragana Gordic/Shutterstock.com, 24; © Nelson Antoine/
Shutterstock.com, 27

Cherry Lake Press is an imprint of Cherry Lake Publishing Group.

Library of Congress Cataloging-in-Publication Data

Names: Knutson, Julie, author.
Title: Do the work! : zero hunger / by Julie Knutson.
Description: Ann Arbor, Michigan : Cherry Lake Publishing, 2022. | Series: Committing to the UN's sustainable
    development goals | Audience: Grades 4-6
Identifiers: LCCN 2021036398 (print) | LCCN 2021036399 (ebook) | ISBN 9781534199248 (hardcover) |
    ISBN 9781668900383 (paperback) | ISBN 9781668906149 (ebook) | ISBN 9781668901823 (pdf)
Subjects: LCSH: Food supply—Juvenile literature. | Hunger—Juvenile literature. | Sustainable agriculture—
    Juvenile literature.
Classification: LCC HD9000.5 .K535 2022 (print) | LCC HD9000.5 (ebook) | DDC 338.1/9—dc23/
    eng/20211014
LC record available at https://lccn.loc.gov/2021036398
LC ebook record available at https://lccn.loc.gov/2021036399

Cherry Lake Publishing Group would like to acknowledge the work of the Partnership for 21st Century
Learning, a Network of Battelle for Kids. Please visit http://www.battelleforkids.org/networks/p21
for more information.

Printed in the United States of America
Corporate Graphics

ABOUT THE AUTHOR

Julie Knutson is an author-educator who writes extensively about global citizenship and the
Sustainable Development Goals. Her previous book, *Global Citizenship: Engage in the Politics
of a Changing World* (Nomad Press, 2020), introduces key concepts about 21st-century
interconnectedness to middle grade and high school readers. She hopes that this series will
inspire young readers to take action and embrace their roles as changemakers in the world.

TABLE OF CONTENTS

CHAPTER 1

Meet the SDGs

Did you know that in today's world, enough food is produced to feed *every* person on the planet? That's right. We actually have all the food we need to feed the world's nearly 8 billion people. But huge numbers of people still experience hunger, **malnutrition**, and **food insecurity** every day.

Why? And what's being done to change this?

A lot of people around the world are working to fight global hunger. They are school children, farmers, food scientists, government workers, and **nonprofit** organizers. They are all united by a common goal—to achieve a world in which all people have enough to eat by 2030. You can join them! Read on to learn how you can help make the **United Nations**' (UN) second **Sustainable** Development Goal (SDG), "Zero Hunger," a reality.

Malnutrition is still the leading cause of death and disease worldwide.

What Are the SDGs?

The SDGs are a set of 17 goals "for people and the planet." They were developed in 2015 and build on an earlier set of goals, the **Millennium** Development Goals. All 191 UN member states have agreed to cooperate in reaching the 169 SDG targets by 2030.

The second goal on the UN's list is "Zero Hunger." Why is this goal so important? How do we define hunger? How does food insecurity relate to the other goals on the list? How can all of us participate in meeting this goal?

Defining Hunger

A sharp pang in your stomach. Feeling tired, grouchy, and lightheaded. A deep desire for food. Hunger is a feeling—a signal from our bodies—that results when we need calories for energy. A balanced, nutritious diet helps keep us healthy. We can focus on school and work. We're less likely to get sick. We grow and thrive.

People don't choose to go hungry. It doesn't result from laziness or lack of effort. It's a problem that results from a lack of opportunity, as well as from unforeseen events and outside forces. A number of hurdles keep people who need food from getting it. Poverty, or not having enough money or resources to meet basic needs, is one root cause. Other causes include food shortages, climate change, war, natural disasters, and food waste.

Worldwide, food insecurity sharply rose as a result of COVID-19. Experts say that the cost of a basic food basket increased by more than 10 percent in 20 countries in the early months of the pandemic. According to the UN, the pandemic caused an increase of up to 270 million people dealing with food insecurity, an 82-percent rise.

END HUNGER, ACHIEVE FOOD SECURITY AND IMPROVED NUTRITION AND PROMOTE SUSTAINABLE AGRICULTURE

BEFORE COVID-19

FOOD INSECURITY WAS ALREADY ON THE RISE

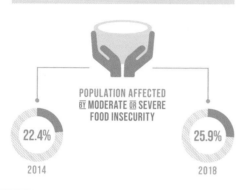

POPULATION AFFECTED BY MODERATE OR SEVERE FOOD INSECURITY

22.4%
2014

25.9%
2018

STUNTING AND WASTING AMONG CHILDREN ARE
LIKELY TO WORSEN

21.3% (144 MILLION)
OF CHILDREN UNDER 5 ARE STUNTED

6.9% (47 MILLION)
OF CHILDREN UNDER 5 ARE AFFECTED BY WASTING
(2019)

COVID-19 IMPLICATIONS

THE PANDEMIC IS AN ADDITIONAL THREAT TO FOOD SYSTEMS

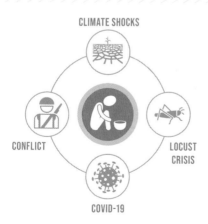

CLIMATE SHOCKS

CONFLICT

LOCUST CRISIS

COVID-19

SMALL-SCALE FOOD PRODUCERS ARE HIT HARD BY THE CRISIS

COMPRISING 40%–85% OF ALL FOOD PRODUCERS IN DEVELOPING REGIONS

SUSTAINABLE DEVELOPMENT G☉ALS

Food, water, and shelter are the basic needs that everyone needs to survive.

Hunger affects people of all ages, all over the world. But certain groups of people are more **vulnerable** to it. Women and girls represent more than 70 percent of people suffering from **chronic** hunger. Hunger and malnutrition impact children's growth and long-term development. Between 2000 and 2017, it was estimated that 22.2 percent of children under 5 had **stunted** growth due to nutritional issues.

What do you think governments should do
to ensure that all people have food?

Food queues are a way of distributing food to people living in poverty. Sometimes these lines can be miles long.

Related Goals

Before we move on, think about hunger in relation to the other goals. Professor Jayashree Arcot of the University of New South Wales in Australia does. Arcot says that solving SDG 1, "No Poverty," will directly help achieve "Zero Hunger," as poverty is a major cause of food insecurity. Creating a world without hunger will also require action on climate change (SDG 13). It will take better **infrastructure** for transporting food and preventing waste (SDGs 9 and 12). It will also need improved access to water (SDG 6) and strategies for ending war and conflict (SDG 16).

Action on SDG 2 will have direct benefits for the health and well-being of millions of people (SDG 3). It will also allow children to develop to their fullest potential, both in and out of the classroom (SDG 4). Let's get started. Keep reading to learn more about how you can help eliminate hunger at home, at school, and in your bigger community!

Hunger in History

Records of food shortages date back to the ancient world. The oldest recorded account of a **famine** is found on an Egyptian **stela**. This message dates from between 332 and 31 BCE. It tells of a 7-year period of drought and starvation during the reign of the pharaoh Djoser.

In more recent history, famine and starvation have caused many cases of global migration. In the 1800s, the Irish Potato Famine led more than 1 million people to emigrate from Ireland to America. That 6-year crisis began in the summer of 1845. An airborne fungus that came to Ireland by way of cargo ships infected and destroyed the country's main crop. More than 1 million people died of starvation during this tragic period.

CHAPTER 2

Why Do We Have Goals?

You've set a goal. Now . . . what's next?

When you want to achieve something, goals are a great first step. But it takes a concrete plan to actually realize them. The authors of the UN SDGs recognize this. That's why they broke them into smaller parts and set up **indicators** to measure success.

STOP AND THINK: *Think about a time when you've set and achieved a goal. What did it take to accomplish it?*

Indicators let you know how far you've come and how close you are to reaching your goal.

SDG 2 centers on building a food system—now and in the future—that is better for people and the planet.

To meet Goal 2, "Zero Hunger," the following will have to be achieved by the year 2030:

- End hunger for all people by ensuring access to safe, nutritious food.
- End malnutrition, and in the process, end childhood **wasting** and stunting.
- Help small-scale farmers, especially women and **Indigenous** farmers, double the amount they produce by 2030.
- Make agriculture more sustainable by strengthening **ecosystems**, plant adaptability, and soil quality.
- Maintain plant diversity.
- Improve infrastructure so that more food gets to people who need it, and less food goes to waste.
- Make changes to food **commodity markets** to prevent major price drops or spikes, which impact farmers and consumers alike.

Genetically modified crops can be made to have greater nutritional value.

If you take a close look at these smaller goals, you'll notice that they're all specific, measurable, achievable, and relevant. They're also timed—a 15-year deadline is set for reaching them. And they're not just about ending hunger. They're also about creating food systems that are fairer and better for the environment, now and in the future.

While you might think these tasks fall on governments alone, there are many things that you can do to help too!

Ready to find out how? Keep reading!

To GMO, or Not to GMO?

Climate change is making farming—and the world's food supply—less stable. At the same time, the global population is growing. There's also less farmable land available. Due to all these factors, scientists are thinking about the future of food. Some support developing more **resilient** plants. These crops would be more adaptable to hot and dry temperatures.

How would this work? Plants would be modified with the gene-editing technology. As author Tom Parrett explained in a 2015 *Newsweek* article, the process "can easily modify plant DNA without changing the plant's essence." While many see this as a promising solution, some consumer and environmental groups say that more safety research is needed.

CHAPTER 3

Do the Work! Contribute to the Goals at Home

We can all perform small actions every day to help reach "Zero Hunger" by 2030. Start at home. Educate your family and friends about the SDGs. Brainstorm about what you can do as a group to address hunger and curb food waste.

In the United States, between 30 and 40 percent of perfectly good food goes to waste. *All* of that food required water to grow, transportation to reach stores, and packaging to be market-ready. SDG 2 centers on being more conscious about what we buy and what we throw away. Tell your family members about this problem. Work together to find ways to make sure that healthy, **perishable** foods land in your stomachs, not in the landfill.

Launch a family book club to continue your learning!

Next time your family is grocery shopping, pick an item to donate.

Beyond curbing food waste and supporting local agriculture, here are some other things you can do to fight hunger from home:

- **Donate Non-Perishable Food** — Food banks always welcome non-perishable items such as cereal and canned soup. Many grocery stores have a collection spot for local food pantries near the registers.

- **Skip the Gifts** — For your next birthday or gift-giving holiday, consider giving rather than getting. Donations to organizations like Feeding America, Action Against Hunger, Oxfam, or World Central Kitchen make a great gift for the whole human family.

- **Talk** — Talk about what you've learned about hunger with your family and friends. Challenge their ideas and opinions about it. Ask them to join you as an ally in fighting hunger in your community and beyond it.

STOP AND THINK: *What can you do to waste less food? Make a list of ideas and post it in your kitchen. This way, all members of your household can see it . . . and add ideas of their own!*

Achieving "Zero Hunger" also hinges on supporting small-scale farmers. Research farmers' markets in your area. Visit with a family member to find local foods that you can bring to your table! You'll be supporting local agriculture and helping to cut "food mile" **carbon emissions**. *A food mile describes the amount of fuel used to transport food 1 mile (1.6 kilometers) between the producer and consumer.*

CHAPTER 4

Do the Work! Contribute to the Goals at School

At schools all across the world, students are taking action on the SDGs. "Feed2Succeed," a nonprofit founded and run by teens, raises funds to sponsor school lunches for children at risk of malnourishment in the Philippines. Interactive events can help your peers see hunger in a new light. Talk to your classmates, teachers, and school administrators about trying out some of the following actions:

- **Food Drives** — Work with your classmates, teachers, and principal to plan a food drive at your school. Find out more about local food pantries and their current needs. Then make your classroom a collection point for these goods.

What other ways can you and your school fight to end hunger?

- **Fundraise** — You can also host a car wash, "fun run," or student craft sale to raise money for groups working for food justice. In 2021, pre-K through fourth-grade students at Springside Chestnut Hill Academy in Philadelphia raised $16,412.05 through their 5K "Race Against Hunger" event! Students wrote letters, crafted pitches, and made posters to inform others about hunger. The money they raised went to two local charities.

Research student-led organizations that fight hunger.

- **Spark Discussion** — Get the conversation about food justice started in your classroom. Research local groups fighting hunger and inequality in the food system. Ask your teacher if your class could host a virtual or in-person guest from the organization to talk about hunger in your community.

   Another way to spark discussion is through events like Oxfam's "Hunger Banquet." On arrival, each person draws a ticket that determines their place at the table. A few guests receive an average meal with meat and fresh vegetables. A bigger group eats a simple meal of rice and beans. The rest of the guests share only a small bowl of rice. The event shows that, just like in real life, your circumstances are determined for you, like how most are born into poverty. According to Oxfam, more than 850,000 people have attended a Hunger Banquet over the past 40 years.

- **Start a Club** — You can launch a volunteer group like Feed2Succeed at your school! What steps does it take to organize a club? Find a faculty sponsor and work with them to find the resources you need to get started. Your club can host fundraising drives, book clubs, and events to raise awareness about hunger.

CHAPTER 5

Do the Work! Contribute to the Goals in Your Community

Got food at risk of waste and in need of rescue? If you live in Pittsburgh, Pennsylvania, call 412 Food Rescue! When quality food needs a home, this organization's volunteer drivers get a "ping!" on the 412 Food Rescue app. Volunteers then pick up the food from locations around the city. Next, the food is redistributed to people in need. The 412 Food Rescue Hero platform has rescued over 20 million pounds (9,071,847.4 kilograms) of food from going to waste since it was established! Today, the broader organization Food Rescue Hero operates in several U.S. cities, from Cleveland, Ohio, to Los Angeles, California.

Was your community impacted by COVID-19?
Some communities hosted food donations during the pandemic.

Kids can join adults as Food Rescue Heroes and at similar organizations around the country. It might involve shelving canned goods at a food pantry. Or it could mean serving breakfast at a homeless shelter. You could pick vegetables at a community garden like Detroit's Pingree Farms, which grows and distributes produce to local people experiencing food insecurity. There are countless ways that you and your family can help address hunger in your community!

> **STOP AND THINK:** *Many activists object to the use of the term "food deserts." They believe the term makes these spaces seem "natural" and shifts attention from the human systems that created these spaces. What name would you suggest as an alternative?*

Write letters to your local newspaper, vlog, or blog to inform other people about food insecurity. Keep educating yourself about the issue by reading books and researching organizations that fight hunger, like Feeding America. Reach out to your elected officials to ask what policies they support to end hunger and build sustainable agriculture. And make *them* aware of the possibilities through programs like Food Rescue Hero.

At home, at school, and in the community at large, you have a voice! Use it to help reach the world's goal of "Zero Hunger" by 2030.

In the United States, many communities of color are considered "food deserts." This means that fresh, affordable, and quality food is not available. Most of the food available is processed, cheap, and unhealthy. In both large cities and rural towns, individuals and groups are calling out this injustice and working to root out racism in our food system.

Extend Your Learning

Background

In November 1990, two Michigan art teachers had an idea. John Hartom's ceramics students were hosting a holiday food drive. Rather than just donate food, he and his wife helped their students make soup bowls. Then they hosted a lunch for the school community, using the student-made bowls to serve the food. A movement was born. Today, people gather for Empty Bowls soup lunches and ice cream socials. At these events, people come together to learn about hunger and donate to local food banks.

Act

With help from an adult, you can plan an Empty Bowls event in your community! Reach out to food banks in your area to tell them you're thinking of hosting an event. They may have some tips for you as you get started.

Then work with your adult helper to get the needed supplies and set a date for your event. Make posters and fliers to tell people about it. Your event may very well inspire your guests to work to wipe out hunger in your city or town!

Further Research

BOOK

Sjonger, Rebecca. *Taking Action to End Poverty.* New York, NY: Crabtree
  Publishing Company, 2019.

WEBSITES

Goal 2: Zero Hunger—United Nations Sustainable Development
https://www.un.org/sustainabledevelopment/hunger
Check out the UN's Sustainable Development Goals website for more
information on Goal 2.

Learn About Hunger—World Hunger Education
www.worldhunger.org/learn-about-hunger
Learn more about hunger and poverty.

The Global Goals of Sustainable Development
margreetdeheer.com/eng/globalgoals.html
Check out these free comics about the UN's Sustainable Development Goals.

Why Is World Hunger Still a Problem?—Wonderopolis
wonderopolis.org/wonder/why-is-world-hunger-still-a-problem
Learn more about hunger and food waste.

Glossary

carbon emissions (KAHR-buhn EE-MIH-shuhns) gases released into the atmosphere that contribute to climate change

chronic (KRAH-nik) long-lasting and difficult to get rid of

commodity markets (kuh-MAH-duh-tee MAHR-kuhts) financial exchange systems with fixed prices for raw materials like corn or soybeans

ecosystems (EE-koh-sih-stuhms) communities of animals and plants interacting with their environments

famine (FAH-muhn) a period of food scarcity

food insecurity (FOOD in-suh-KYOOR-ih-tee) not having reliable access to nutritious and affordable food

indicators (in-duh-KAY-tuhrs) measurements of progress

Indigenous (in-DIH-juh-nuhss) native to a place

infrastructure (IN-fruh-struhk-chuhr) basic physical and operational needs for society to operate, such as roads and bridges

malnutrition (mal-noo-TRIH-shuhn) lacking proper nutrition

millennium (muh-LEH-nee-uhm) a period of 1,000 years

nonprofit (nahn-PRAH-fuht) an organization that does not seek to make a profit

perishable (PAHR-ih-shuh-buhl) food that can spoil easily

resilient (rih-ZIL-yuhnt) able to recover after a disaster or catastrophe

stela (STEE-luh) an upright stone slab or column

stunted (STUHN-tuhd) interrupted growth, specifically, height

sustainable (suh-STAY-nuh-buhl) able to be maintained at a certain rate

United Nations (yuh-NYE-tuhd NAY-shuhns) the international organization that promotes peace and cooperation among nations

vulnerable (VUHL-nuh-ruh-buhl) susceptible to harm

wasting (WAY-sting) causing part of the body to become weak and frail

INDEX